Receiving Peace

a journaling encounter

Receiving Peace

a journaling encounter

Margaret Lehman

Ocala, Florida

Published by Bright Ridge Publishing in 2020
First edition, First printing

Copyright ©2020 Margaret Lehman
All rights reserved.

www.IntimateAwe.com

Scriptures marked ESV are taken from the English Standard Version ©2001, 2007, 2011, 2016 by Crossway Books and Bibles, a Publishing Ministry of Good News Publishers.

Scriptures marked NKJV are taken from the New King James Version ©1982 by Thomas Nelson, Inc.

Scriptures marked NIV are taken from the New International Version ©1973, 1978, 1984, 2011 by Biblica, Inc.

Scriptures marked NASB are taken from the New American Standard Bible ©1960, 1962, 1963, 1968, 1971, 1972, 1973, 1975, 1977, 1995 by The Lockman Foundation, La Habra, Calif.

Scriptures marked NLT are taken from the New Living Translation ©1996, 2004, 2007 by Tyndale House Publishers Inc., Carol Stream, IL 60188

Cover background image by Manfred Richter from pixabay.com

No part of this book may be reproduced or transmitted in any form or by any means, including but not limited to information storage and retrieval systems, electronic, mechanical, photocopy, recording, etc. without written permission from the copyright holder.

ISBN 978-1-7353478-0-6

Dedication

*To the ladies of the JOY program,
may you be receivers and agents
of God's great peace*

Contents

Introduction:

What Is a Journaling Encounter?........................11

About Peace...12

How to Use This Book..................................14

A Note for Small-Group Use............................16

1. The Source of Peace................................17

2. The Promise of Peace...............................29

3. The Obstacles to Peace.............................41

4. The Person of Peace................................53

5. The Benefits of Peace..............................75

6. The Power of Peace................................105

7. The Rule of Peace.................................119

8. The Blessing of Peace.............................129

Appendix: List of Blessings of Peace from Scripture..........138

Introduction

What Is a Journaling Encounter?

Life is a journey. It isn't static. We learn and grow and become in the process of living. Every relationship and every circumstance provide another thread in the story line. Some for joy, some for overcoming. Some for shaping, some for being shaped.

Life is also a quest. It is not without goal. There are some things we are searching for. Our innate sense of discovery drives us to answer big-picture questions about identity and purpose and meaning. And to search out solutions for our own individual puzzles in all their shapes and sizes.

Journey and quest. Process and product. A big adventure.

Both can be honed by some intentional focus. And that is the invitation inherent in this journal. The King invites you to search out truth and apply it to your journey. The Master Teacher Himself welcomes you with the words, "Learn from Me," (Matthew 11:29) and offers you a position beside Him on the road.

This book is meant to be a tool that helps bring into focus whatever He is teaching you on this leg of the trek.

As you read and pray, you will be writing your own book on peace. These pages will hold the record of your journey as you watch, consider, question, express, respond, and implement the substance of your conversations with God.

His fingerprints are everywhere around for those willing to pay attention. And He communicates in a thousand different ways. He wants you to seek. And He wants you to find Him. Enjoy both the process and the discoveries.

You're not turning this book in for a grade. In fact, nobody else ever has to see it. So give yourself permission to make stick figures, draw doodles, and cobble words together, however simplistic and primitive it may feel.

This is, quite literally, just some created space to give you room to interact with Him.

May your journey be blessed with encountering God Himself in a way that transforms you forever.

About Peace

A medical diagnosis. Family conflict. Memories of abuse. Depression. Business failure. Pandemic. Daily overwhelm. Breaking news, or news that breaks us. I don't need to exhaust the list. We all know first-hand that the world is marred. And at any moment along comes a trigger to remind us we need peace.

It's easy to think of peace as the absence of problems. "If this were fixed, I would be OK."

God absolutely intervenes in the conflicts of our lives. He's been taking the initiative to rescue, deliver, and save since mankind's first self-inflicted distress in the Garden. And He hasn't changed.

But sometimes in the circumstances of our life stories, He goes for the greater miracle—the deeper peace of calming us before resolving our dilemma. Instead of leveling the mountain, He gives us feet that enable us to stand on the heights like a sure-footed mountain goat (Psalm 18:33). I want those feet.

Sometimes God enforces peace. Put your head around those two seemingly contradictory concepts. We have a God who will fight for us. We also have a God who is not intimidated by any amount of conflict required to establish peace, to make peace, to forge peace. Sometimes productive pain is involved in the process of getting to peace. Just look at the cross to see the lengths to which He will go to make peace for us. He is a Warrior to the death...and over death.

The biblical notion of peace encompasses much more than a successful end to whatever irritant we feel most acutely.

Let me illustrate it this way. In September 2017, Hurricane Irma barreled across the Caribbean, growing into a monster Category 5 storm before it turned north to train its sights on the whole of Florida.

Damage to homes, businesses, and crops was considerable in many places, and about 73% of the state lost electricity at some point.

Our home was completely spared, and our city suffered surprisingly little damage. But our house had no power or water for the next seven days.

Because the dialysis center did have electricity for my father-in-law's visits, a week of indoor camping fell into the category of inconvenience more than hardship. We had experienced peace through a literal storm and knew that in a matter of time, we'd have electricity again too. Much to be thankful for and nothing to complain over.

Tropical storms, though, are hot and sticky events. High humidity without fans or AC means you will be sleeping with the windows open.

The neighbor ran a generator for those seven days, which was parked right outside our bedroom window. It droned. It grated.

I will never forget the glorious moment that Sunday afternoon when it stopped. Blissful quiet. "Peace." My whole body relaxed.

My first thought was of enjoying the silence. But that silence was a sign. It pointed to something. The generator stopped because the electricity was back on. The bigger "peace" was that all had been restored to proper functioning. The sound was peaceful but the signal even more so.

The biblical idea of peace is like that. Much more than a ceasefire to a war, peace is an all-encompassing wholeness. Peace is about things being set "right." Peace is that well-being on every level and in every facet of life.

Peace is part of the nature of God. Everything about Him is whole and right and in place. And that's why trying to find peace apart from the God Who IS Peace is a logical impossibility.

The good news is that He delights to give His peace to us. He gives us Himself, and peace is part of the package of that shared relationship.

You are invited on a journey that no one else can take for you. May this journal provide the space for your next steps of hearing and responding to the Voice who speaks peace, gives peace, and makes peace because He IS peace.

I bless you to discover and rest in the God of Peace.

How to Use This Book

Each two-page spread contains the day's focus verse, space to respond, and a blessing.

The Focus Verse
Read the verse several times and think about what God is saying. Ask the Holy Spirit to teach you what He wants you to understand about Himself and about you. For more thorough study, read the verses around the focus verse in your own Bible to get a sense of the context in which it was spoken. There are lots of free Bible study tools available online these days that you can use to look up definitions of words, compare translations, and dig as deep as you want to go. Take enough time to "chew" on the words and savor truth that is rock-solid enough to build your life on.

The Sketch Box
- You can draw, color, sketch, doodle, or cartoon in any manner you want to illustrate what you're contemplating. If some kind of picture comes to mind as you are praying and meditating, even roughly sketching it out will help you remember it later.
- If you don't want to draw, you could write a single word or phrase with artful lettering.
- Copy the focus verse if that would help you memorize it.
- Add pictures from other sources: Take and print some photos from your phone (You'll be surprised at the things you start noticing in nature and daily life as you work through the book. Capture it and include it). Download clip art from your computer. Or cut and paste (the old-school way) from a magazine.
- Do certain colors of paint swatches from the home improvement store, or certain textures of fabric samples remind you of peace? Glue them in.
- Press a flower, or add a feather. Be creative like the God in whose image you are made!

The Blank Lines

The simplest way to figure out what to write about is to pose this question to yourself: "God has just spoken this truth to me. What do I want to say back to Him?"

- Write out your prayer to Him.
- Make a list of questions you have or observations you made.
- Copy the verse to help you memorize it.
- Create bullet points of ways you'd like to respond or take action on this truth.

Above all, make it personal. This is not a dutiful exercise. It is your opportunity to connect with the King. He's looking forward to your time together. Are you?

The Blessing

Sometimes the best way to pray is just to say God's truth back to Him. We can also pray from these verses for others. And we can speak them as blessings, which is how I have written them for you. It is my earnest desire that He blesses you more than you could have imagined through this process. May your peace be great!

A Note for Small-Group Use

One of the most transformational small groups I ever participated in used the following format: Each member committed to five one-on-one meetings with God per week, during which we read some Scripture and journaled about it. When we came together, each person shared something they had gleaned during the week. Some read directly from their journals; others just talked about their "nugget." Then we prayed for each other. It was simple, and it was rich.

This book is suitable for a similar format that you could schedule as an 11-week study. After the introductory meeting, complete a chapter per week. But plan to spend two weeks on "The Person of Peace," and three weeks on "The Benefits of Peace" (that is, 5 entries per week).

Even if you only meet with one other person, sharing the treasures you've found will both enrich each other and help to cement the things you discovered.

The Source
of Peace

But the LORD said to him, "Peace be to you. Do not fear; you shall not die." Then Gideon built an altar there to the LORD and called it, The LORD Is Peace.

Judges 6:23-24 ESV

I bless you in the name of the One who reveals Himself as "The Lord IS Peace."

The LORD lift up His countenance upon you, and give you peace.

Numbers 6:26 NKJV

May you know the peace that comes from the Lord's face shining on you.

"I form the light and create darkness.
I make peace and create calamity;
I, the LORD, do all these things."

Isaiah 45:7 NKJV

May you be in awe of His creative power to fashion peace as magnificently as He created light.

"I will make a covenant of peace with them. It shall be an everlasting covenant with them. And I will set them in their land and multiply them, and will set my sanctuary in their midst forevermore."

Ezekiel 37:26 ESV

May you know to your core that you have a refuge of peace because He Himself has come to dwell with us.

Grace and peace
be multiplied to you in the
knowledge of God and
of Jesus our Lord.

2 Peter 1:2 NKJV

I bless you with grace and peace in abundance as you know Him more and more.

The Promise of Peace

LORD, you establish peace for us;
all that we have accomplished
you have done for us.

Isaiah 26:12 NIV

May you anchor to the peace He has established for you.

For unto us a Child is born,
Unto us a Son is given;
And the government will be
upon His shoulder.
And His name will be called
Wonderful, Counselor, Mighty God,
Everlasting Father,
Prince of Peace.

Isaiah 9:6 NKJV

I bless you in the name of the One who rules as the Prince of Peace.

How beautiful upon the mountains
are the feet of him who brings good news,
who publishes peace,
who brings good news of happiness,
who publishes salvation, who says to Zion,
"Your God reigns!"

Isaiah 52:7 ESV

I bless you with the peace of the announcement that your God sits as King forever.

"I create the fruit of the lips:
Peace, peace to him who is far off
and to him who is near," says the LORD,
"And I will heal him."

Isaiah 57:19 NKJV

I bless you to hear Him declaring peace to you... no matter where you are.

And He came and preached peace
to you who were far away,
and peace to those who were near;
for through Him
we both have our access in one Spirit
to the Father.

Ephesians 2:17-18 NASB

May you experience the peace that gives you access to the God of heaven.

The Obstacles to Peace

"There is no peace,"
says the LORD, "for the wicked."

Isaiah 48:22 ESV

I bless you with perspective and truth about where peace is found and where it isn't.

"If only you had paid attention to my
commands, your peace would have been
like a river,
your well-being like the waves
of the sea."

Isaiah 48:18 NIV

May you position yourself to feel the flow of peace like a river.

For to set the mind on the flesh is death,
but to set the mind on the Spirit
is life and peace.

Romans 8:6 ESV

May you know the peace of a mind that is aligned with the Spirit.

For the kingdom of God is not a
matter of eating and drinking,
but of righteousness,
peace and joy in the Holy Spirit.

>Romans 14:17 NIV

I bless you to pursue those things that are life indeed and to be satisfied with nothing less.

The acts of the flesh are obvious...
But the fruit of the Spirit is
love, joy, peace...

Galatians 5:19,22 NIV

May the fruit of peace be produced in you by the power of the Holy Spirit.

The Person of Peace

He has come!

To give light to those who sit in darkness
and in the shadow of death,
To guide our feet into the way of peace.

Luke 1:79 NKJV

I bless you to walk out of darkness into His path of peace.

"Glory to God in the highest heaven,
and on earth peace
to those on whom his favor rests."

Luke 2:14 NIV

May your heart hear afresh the angels' announcement of good news for you.

But he was pierced for our transgressions,
he was crushed for our iniquities;
the punishment that brought us peace
was on him, and
by his wounds we are healed.

Isaiah 53:5 NIV

I bless you to stand in awe of the One who purchased your salvation. His punishment on the cross brought you peace and healed your wounds.

For He Himself is our peace, who made both groups into one and broke down the barrier of the dividing wall by abolishing in His flesh the enmity, which is the Law of commandments contained in ordinances, so that in Himself He might make the two into one new man, thus establishing peace, and might reconcile them in one body to God through the cross, by it having put to death the enmity.

Ephesians 2:14-16 NASB

May you find peace with God and with others through the power of Jesus' blood given for you on the cross.

Therefore, since we have been
justified by faith,
we have peace with God
through our Lord Jesus Christ.

Romans 5:1 ESV

May you know the peace of being declared "not guilty" before a righteous God.

This is the message of Good News for the
people of Israel–that there is peace
with God through Jesus Christ,
who is Lord of all.

Acts 10:36 NLT

May you receive peace from the One who is Lord of all.

And through him God reconciled everything to himself.
He made peace with everything in heaven and on earth by means of Christ's blood on the cross.

Colossians 1:20 NLT

I bless you with the peace of His blood that reconciled ALL things.

Then He arose and rebuked the wind,
and said to the sea,
"Peace, be still!"
And the wind ceased and there was
a great calm.

                        Mark 4:39 NKJV

*I bless you with the presence of the One who speaks peace to the sea—
and it obeys.*

Eight days later, his disciples were inside again, and Thomas was with them. Although the doors were locked, Jesus came and stood among them and said, "Peace be with you."

John 20:26 ESV

I bless you to hear the resurrected Christ saying to you, "Peace be with you."

And He said to her,
"Daughter, your faith has made you well;
go in peace."

Luke 8:48 ESV

May you hear your Savior-Healer-Redeemer saying to you, "Go in peace."

The Benefits of Peace

"Peace I leave with you.
My peace I give to you;
not as the world gives do I give to you.
Let not your heart be troubled,
neither let it be afraid."

John 14:27 NKJV

I bless you with the peace Jesus left for you. May you receive the peace He gives. I bless you with a heart that is not troubled or afraid.

All your children shall be taught by the LORD, and great shall be the peace of your children.

Isaiah 54:13 NKJV

May you see His peace extended to the next generation.

In peace I will both lie down and sleep;
for you alone, O LORD,
make me dwell in safety.

Psalm 4:8 ESV

*May you be
blessed with both
the fact
of security
and the feeling
of safety.*

Steadfast love and faithfulness meet;
righteousness and peace
kiss each other.

Psalm 85:10 ESV

I bless you with the peace that is coupled with righteousness in the place where love and faithfulness come together.

And the effect of righteousness
will be peace,
and the result of righteousness,
quietness and assurance forever.

Isaiah 32:17 NKJV

May His righteousness result in your having peace, quietness, and confidence forever.

Great peace have those who
love your law;
nothing can make them stumble.

Psalm 119:165 ESV

May you know the peace that comes with cooperating with the rule of His laws and principles.

Her [Wisdom's] ways are ways of pleasantness,
And all her paths are peace.

Proverbs 3:17 NKJV

I bless you to know His pleasant ways and His paths of peace in wisdom.

"Peace be within your walls and security within your towers!"
For my brothers and companions' sake I will say, "Peace be within you!"

Psalm 122:7-8 ESV

May there be peace within your walls and security in your house. Peace be within you.

A heart at peace
gives life to the body,
but envy rots the bones.

Proverbs 14:30 NIV

May your heart be at peace and give life to your body.

You keep him in perfect peace
whose mind is stayed on you,
because he trusts in you.

Isaiah 26:3 ESV

I bless you with perfect peace, a steadfast mind, and a trusting heart.

"So do not be afraid, Jacob my servant;
do not be dismayed, Israel,"
declares the LORD,
"I will surely save you out of a distant
place, your descendants from the land of
their exile. Jacob will again have peace
and security, and no one will make
him afraid."

                                      Jeremiah 30:10 NIV

May your land be at rest, and may His peace bring security so that you are not afraid.

He makes peace in your borders,
And fills you with the finest wheat.

Psalm 147:14 NKJV

I bless you with secure boundaries, rest within, and the fullness of His provision.

"For the mountains shall depart,
And the hills be removed, but My kindness shall not depart from you,
Nor shall My covenant of peace be removed," says the LORD, who has mercy on you.

Isaiah 54:10 NKJV

I bless you to know that God keeps His covenant of peace. His unfailing love cannot be shaken. He has compassion on you.

For I know the thoughts I think
toward you, says the LORD,
thoughts of peace and not of evil,
to give you a future
and a hope.

Jeremiah 29:11 NKJV

I bless you to delight in a God who is thinking about you and planning peace.

The Power of Peace

He has redeemed my soul in peace
from the battle that was against me,
For there were many against me.

Psalm 55:18 NKJV

May you know the rescue and victory of His peace.

And, as shoes for your feet,
having put on the readiness given by the
gospel of peace.

Ephesians 6:15 ESV

I bless you to stand armed with the peace of the good news of the Gospel.

When the LORD takes pleasure in anyone's way, he causes even their enemies to make peace with them.

Proverbs 16:7 NIV

May His peace be so strong in your life that even those who oppose you are affected by it.

"I have said these things to you,
that in me you may have peace.
In the world you will have tribulation.
But take heart;
I have overcome the world."

John 16:33 ESV

I bless you to walk in a broken world with courage and peace because the One who overcame the world walks with you.

Therefore let us pursue the
things which make for peace
and the things by which
one may edify another.

Romans 14:19 NKJV

I bless you to pursue peace, experience it, spread it, and build others with it.

The God of peace will soon crush Satan under your feet. The grace of our Lord Jesus Christ be with you.

Romans 16:20 ESV

May the God of peace crush Satan under your feet.

The Rule
of Peace

And let the peace of Christ rule in your hearts, to which indeed you were called in one body. And be thankful.

Colossians 3:15 ESV

May His peace be the umpire that decides, directs, and call the shots in your life.

Instead of bronze I will bring you gold, and silver in place of iron. Instead of wood I will bring you bronze, and iron in place of stones. I will make peace your governor and well-being your ruler.

Isaiah 60:17 NIV

May His peace rule and govern in this place.

For God is not the author of confusion but of peace...

1 Corinthians 14:33 NKJV

I bless you with the order and alignment that come from His peace.

And the peace of God,
which surpasses all understanding,
will guard your hearts and minds
through Christ Jesus.

Philippians 4:7 NKJV

May His peace stand as the sentry protecting your heart and mind.

The Blessing of Peace

May God himself, the God of peace,
sanctify you through and through.
May your whole spirit, soul and body
be kept blameless at the coming
of our Lord Jesus Christ.

1 Thessalonians 5:23 NIV

May the God of peace sanctify your spirit, soul, and body.

Now may the God of hope fill you with all joy and peace in believing, that you may abound in hope by the power of the Holy Spirit.

Romans 15:13 NKJV

May the God of hope fill you with peace.

Now may the Lord of peace Himself
continually grant you peace
in every circumstance.
The Lord be with you all!

2 Thessalonians 3:16 NASB

In every time and every place, may He give you His peace.

...Grace and peace to you from the one who is, who always was, and who is still to come; from the sevenfold Spirit before his throne; and from Jesus Christ. He is the faithful witness to these things, the first to rise from the dead, and the ruler of all the kings of the world...

Revelation 1:4-5 NLT

May you receive peace from the throne of the eternal, complete, triune, and only God.

Blessings of Peace from the Scriptures

I bless you with the peace that comes from the Lord's face shining on you. Num. 6:26

I bless you through the One named "The LORD is Peace," Judg. 6:24 the One who rules as Prince of Peace. Is. 9:6

I bless you with peace that lets you lie down and rest, that lets you dwell in safety. Ps. 4:8

I bless you with the peace that is coupled with righteousness in the place where love and faithfulness come together. Ps. 85:10

May you know the peace that comes in cooperating with the rule of His laws and His principles. Ps. 119:165

May there be peace within your walls. Security in your house. Peace be within you. Ps. 122:7-8

I bless you to know His pleasant ways and His paths of peace in wisdom. Prov. 3:17 May He guide your feet into the path of peace. Luke 1:79

May your heart be at peace and give life to your body. Prov. 14:30

I bless you with perfect peace, a steadfast mind, and a trusting heart that knows He has established peace for you. Is. 26:3,12

May the fruit of peace be produced in you by the righteousness of Christ Eph. 2:15 and the power of the Holy Spirit Gal. 5:22, granting you quietness and confidence forever. Is. 32:17

I bless you to feel the flow of peace like a river. Is. 48:18, Is. 66:12

I bless you to know that God keeps His covenant of peace. His unfailing love cannot be shaken. He has compassion on you. Is. 54:10

Grace and peace be yours in abundance. 1 Pet. 1:2

May His peace rule and govern in this place. Is. 60:17 May His peace bring security so that NO ONE is afraid. Jer. 30:10 His sanctuary, His refuge of peace is here among us. Ezek. 37:26

I bless you with the peace of the good news of the Gospel. Eph. 6:15 It declares, "Our God reigns!" Is. 52:7 He purchased our salvation when He was pierced for our transgressions. His punishment on the cross brought us peace and healed our wounds. Is. 53:5 He Himself IS our peace. Eph. 2:14

The Lord declares peace to those far away and near. And He will heal. Is. 57:19 Eph. 2:17

I bless you with the peace Jesus left you. I bless you with the peace He gives you. It is not like the world gives. I bless you with a heart that is not troubled or afraid. John 14:27

I bless you to hear Jesus saying, "Peace be with you!" and "Go in peace." May you hear these as the words of the Resurrected Christ Jn.20:26, the Savior Lk. 8:48, the Lord of all. Acts 10:36

May you know the peace of being justified by faith. Rom. 5:1

May you know the peace of a mind governed by the Spirit. Rom. 8:6

May the God of hope fill you with peace. Rom. 15:13

May the God of peace crush Satan under your feet. Rom. 16:20

I bless you with the order and alignment that come from His peace. 1 Cor. 14:33

May His peace guard your heart and your mind. Phil. 4:7

I bless you with the peace of His blood, shed on the cross, that reconciled all things. Col. 1:20

May the God of peace sanctify your spirit, soul, and body. 1 Thess. 5:23

May the Lord of peace Himself give you peace at all times in every way. 2 Thess. 3:16

About the Author

Margaret Lehman is a friend alongside on the journey of faith and a worshiper of Jesus. She celebrates the awe and delight of meeting an extraordinary God in the everyday moments of life. And she loves it when His mercy and power meet us in our brokenness to write a better ending to our stories.

She has worked as a freelance writer and editor, taught writing classes and Bible studies, and homeschooled for more years than she can count. She and her husband have five daughters and live in north central Florida.

You may contact Margaret at www.IntimateAwe.com.

www.ingramcontent.com/pod-product-compliance
Lightning Source LLC
Chambersburg PA
CBHW071352080526
44587CB00017B/3072